103 St Patricks Day Jokes For Kids

The Lucky Saint Patrick's Day Joke Book For Boys And Girls

Association and a Committee of Publishers and Associations.

In no way is it legal to reproduce, duplicate, or transmit any part of this document by either electronic means or in printed format. Recording of this publication is strictly prohibited and any storage of this document is not allowed unless with written permission from the publisher. All rights reserved.

The information provided herein is stated to be truthful and consistent, in that any liability, in terms of inattention or otherwise, by any usage or abuse of any policies, processes, or directions

Q: Why can't you borrow money from a leprechaun?

A: Because they're always a little short.

Q: Why should you never iron a 4 leaf clover?

A: Because you don't want to press your luck!

Knock Knock

Who's there?

Irish.

Irish who?

Irish you a happy St. Patrick's Day!

I said to my friend, "I know a girl who married an Irishman on St. Patrick's Day."

He said "Oh really?"

I said "No, O'Reilly!"

A tourist is in Cork but wants to go to Dublin for the St. Patrick's Day celebrations. He stops Paddy in the street and asks him, "Excuse me, can you tell me the quickest way to Dublin?"

Paddy says "Are you on foot or driving by car?"

The tourist replies "By car".

Paddy says "Good, that's the quickest way!"

Q: How can you tell if an Irishman is having a good time?

A: He's Dublin over with laughter.

Q: Why don't women want to get engaged on St. Patrick's Day?

A: Because they don't want to get a "sham rock"

Q: How is a good friend like a 4 leaf clover?

A: They're both hard to find and lucky to have.

Knock, knock.

Who's there?

Boy.

Boy who?

Boy do I love St. Paddy's Day!

Knock, knock.

Who's there?

Clover.

Clover who?

Clover here and I'll tell you.

Q: What position do leprechauns play on a baseball team?

A: Shortstop

Q: Why did the leprechaun cross the road?

A: To get to the pot of gold!

Q: What does Ireland have a lot of?

A: Irish people

Knock, knock.

Who's there?

Aaron.

Aaron who?

Aaron go bragh!

Knock, knock.

Who's there?

Don.

Don who?

Don be puttin' down the Irish.

Q: What is long and green and only shows up once a year?

A: The St. Patrick's Day parade

Q: What did the leprechaun say on March 17?

A: Irish you a Happy St. Patrick's Day.

Q: What is a yadkcirtapts?

A: St Patricks Day spelled backwards.

Q: Why do leprechauns make such good secretaries?

A: They're great at shorthand.

Q: How did the leprechaun beat everyone else to the pot of gold?

A: He took a short cut!

Q: What do you call a big spider in Ireland?

A: Paddy long legs!

Knock, Knock

Who's there?

Erin.

Erin who?

Erin as fast as I could but couldn't catch the leprechaun.

Knock Knock

Who's there?

Ireland.

Ireland who?

Ireland you money if you promise to pay me back.

Q: Why did the leprechaun stand on the potato?

A: To stop himself from falling into the Irish stew.

Q: Why are leprechauns so hard to get with?

A: Because they're very short tempered.

Q: What would you get if you crossed Kris Kringle with St. Patrick?

A: Saint O'Claus

Q: What happened when St. Patrick fell into the Shannon river?

A: He got wet.

Q: What did the leprechaun call the happy man wearing green?

A: A Jolly Green Giant!

Knock Knock

Who's there?

Ireland.

Ireland who?

Ire land you a time-out, so be nice.

Knock, knock.

Who's there?

Irish.

Irish who?

Irish I could find a 4-leaf clover.

Knock, knock.

Who's there?

Irish stew.

Irish stew who?

Irish stew in the name of the law.

Q: What stays out all night at St. Patrick's house?

A: His Paddy O'furniture

Q: Where can you always find gold on St. Patrick's Day?

A: In the dictionary!

Q: What do you call a fake diamond on St. Patrick's Day?

A: A sham rock

Q: What does it mean when you find a horse shoe on St. Patrick's Day?

A: That someone's horse is walking around with only 3 shoes!

Q: What do you call leprechauns who collect cans and plastic?

A: Wee-cyclers!

Q: What was St. Patrick's favorite kind of music?

A: Sham-rock and roll

Knock, knock.

Who's there?

Leper.

Leper who?

Leper con and I'm here to pinch you.

Knock, knock.

Who's there?

Pat.

Pat who?

Pat your coat on – let's go to the St. Patrick's Day parade.

Knock, knock.

Who's there?

Potto.

Potto who?

Potto gold.

Knock, knock.

Who's there?

Rain.

Rain who?

Rainbow leads to a pot o' gold.

Knock, knock.

Who's there?

Saint.

Saint who?

Saint no time for questions, open the door!

Q: What do leprechauns love to barbecue?

A: Short ribs

Q: What musical instrument do show-off musicians play on St. Patrick's Day?

A: They play on their brag-pipes.

Q: How do you describe someone who is jealous of St. Patrick?

A: They're green with envy.

Q: Why do leprechauns like to recycle?

A: So they can stay green.

Q: Why did the leprechaun climb the rainbow?

A: To get to the other slide.

Q: Why do frogs like Saint Patrick's Day?

A: Because they're already wearing green.

Q: What is it called when you do the wrong Irish dance?

A: A jig mistake

Q: What type of bow can't be tied?

A: A rain-bow

Q: Why do leprechauns prefer dollar bills over coins?

A: Because they're green.

Q: Why did the leprechaun turn down the bowl of potato chowder?

A: He already had a pot of gold.

Q: What did one Irish ghost say to the other Irish ghost?

A: Top o' the moaning to you!

Q: What job did the leprechaun have at the restaurant?

A: He was a short-order cook.

Q: Why did the leprechaun go outside?

A: To sit on his Paddy-o.

Q: Why do leprechauns hate sports?

A: They prefer jigging than jogging.

Knock, knock.

Who's there?

Shepherd.

Shepherd who?

Shepherd spy is watching you…

Knock, Knock

Who's there?

Warren

Warren who?

Warren anything green today?

Q: Why does the River Shannon have so much money in it?

A: Because it has 2 banks.

Q: When isn't an Irish potato an Irish potato?

A: When it's a French fry!

Q: Why are so many leprechauns gardeners?

A: They have green thumbs!

Q: What did the Irish potato say to his sweetheart?

A: I have fries only for you.

Q: What do you get when you cross four leaf clovers with poison ivy?

A: A big rash of good luck

Q: What did St. Patrick order to drink at the Chinese restaurant?

A: Green tea

Q: Who was St. Patrick's favorite super hero?

A: Green Lantern

Q: When does Valentine's Day come after St. Patrick's Day?

A: In the dictionary

Q: What did the baby find at the end of the rainbow?

A: A potty of gold

Q: Why was the leprechaun start going to the gym?

A: He wanted to look like the Hulk!

Q: What's a leprechaun's favorite cereal?

A: Lucky Charms

Q: How did St. Patrick light up the field when the power went out during the night game?

A: With a soccer match

Q: What did the leprechaun referee say when the soccer match ended?

A: Game clover!

Q: Why are the Irish so concerned about global warming?

A: They're into living green.

Q: Why can't leprechaun golfers ever end a game?

A: Because they refuse to leave the green!

Q: What's big and purple and lies next to Ireland?

A: Grape Britain

Q: What would you get if you crossed a leprechaun with a Texan?

A: A pot of chilli at the end of the rainbow.

Q: Why do leprechauns hide behind 4-leafclovers and not 3-leafclovers?

A: Because they need all the luck they can get.

Q: What do you get when you do the Irish jig at McDonalds?

A: A Shamrock shake

Q: Where do leprechauns buy their groceries?

A: Rainbow Foods

Q: What is a nuahcerpel?

A: Leprechaun spelled backwards.

Q: What did the leprechaun say to the elf?

A: "How's the weather up there?"

Q: What do you get when two leprechauns have a conversation?

A: Lots of small talk!

Q: What did one Irish cook say to the other?

A: "What do you think about my Gaelic?"

Q: Why do leprechauns have pots of gold?

A: They like to "go" first class.

Q: Do leprechauns get angry when you make fun of their height?

A: Yes, but only a little.

Q: Why did the man cross the road on St. Patrick's day?

A: Because there was a leprechaun on the other side with a pot of gold!

Q: When does the leprechaun cross the road?

A: When the light is green.

Q: What does it mean when you find a horseshoe?

A: A poor horse is going barefoot!

Q: What would you get if you crossed a leprechaun with a frog?

A: A little man having a hopping good time

Q: Why did St. Patrick drive all the snakes out of Ireland?

A: He couldn't get them airfare!

Q: Why do frogs and alligators like St. Patrick's Day?

A: Because they're already wearing green.

Q: What kind of coin did the leprechaun put in the vending machine?

A: A lepre-coin

Q: What did the leprechauns use to get to the moon?

A: A sham-rocket

Q: What do you call a leprechaun's vacation home?

A: A lepre-condo

Q: Why didn't the leprechaun mind ending up in jail?

A: One set of bars was as good as another.

Q: How does Ireland have so many people?

A: Because the capital's always Dublin!

Q: Where would you find a leprechaun baseball team?

A: In the Little League

Q: How did the Irish jig get started?

A: Too much water to drink and not enough restrooms!

Q: Why do you wear green on St. Patrick's Day?

A: So your face will match your clothes after you've been eating and dancing!

Q: What's a leprechaun's favorite drink?

A: Mountain Dew

Q: Which leprechaun has the biggest shoes?

A: The one with the biggest feet!

Q: What would you get if you crossed a dog with an Irish instrument?

A: A bagpup

Q: What do you call a musical performance done by leprechauns?

A: A lepre-concert!

Q: What would you get if you crossed a leprechaun with a frog?

A: Lots of green with a croak of gold

Made in the USA
Lexington, KY
12 March 2019